Leon's Share

Question & Answer/Activity Book

Leon's Share

Question & Answer/Activity Book

By

Mabel Elizabeth Singletary

The Young Conquerors Series

Book 1

Leon's Share
Question & Answer/Activity Book
©Copyright 2013 Mabel E. Singletary

ISBN: 978-0-9886553-1-7

Subject heading: LEON'S SHARE QUESTION & ANSWER ACTIVITY BOOK

Printed in the United States of America

Introduction

Stories of hope and encouragement written for children can have a positive effect and a long lasting impact on the youngsters who read them. This question & answer/activity book was developed and designed to promote discussions about the chapter contents of *Leon's Share* which is book one in *The Young Conquerors Series.*

The activities presented here can act as a guide that will allow readers to comment and assess the story while participating in on going related language arts skills and activities. This workbook can be utilized for small group instruction as well as serve as a useful tool to promote reading for pleasure in recreational book club settings.

Leon's Share

Somebody's got a Secret

1. Did Leon enjoy the attention he got for misbehaving? Explain.
2. Describe Mrs. Kelso. Would you like to have a teacher like her? Explain.
3. How did the laughter of the other students encourage Leon to entertain them?
4. What kind of student is Keith Porter?
5. Would you risk losing your recess to tell a joke? Explain.
6. Do you think ignoring Leon was the right thing for Keith to do? Explain.
7. What kind of relationship does Leon have with his grandfather?
8. Does Leon really have a secret? What is it?

Chapter 1 Activity: *Choose and complete one of the activities below.*

A) Draw and color a scene from chapter one. Give your scene a caption which summarizes and describes an event in the chapter.

B) Set a timer and make as many words as you can from the word *"performance"*. Share the list you created.

C) Divide the following words into syllables: *attention, encourage, ignore, laughter, misbehave, secret.* Choose 3 of the words above and use them in sentences of your own.

Leon's Share

Q & A

Chapter 2

A Different Kind of Show

1. Why did Leon enjoy being in Mrs. Kelso's class?
2. Does Leon love Pop and Nana? How do you know that he does/doesn't?
3. Do you think Leon cares about his grades? Explain.
4. How do you know Leon lacks confidence about his poetry?
5. Why didn't Leon want to share his poem?
6. Why don't Leon and Keith Porter get along?
7. How did Leon feel when Mrs. Kelso said his poem was beautiful?
8. Would you have shared your poem with the class? Why or Why not?

Chapter 2 Activity: *Choose and complete one of the activities below.*

A) Write the following vocabulary words in alphabetical order.

commotion, opportunity, blank, determine, promise, comfortable, gesture, bombshell, whisper, excellence, entire, contained, refold, eagerly, clipped, announce, assignment, composition, grabbed, remind, complain, crumpled, except, pretend, terrain, humiliated, grind, attention, braced, performance, remember, scenery, convince, exhaled, serious, creator, literary, exceptional, verse, reassure.

B) Using the vocabulary words listed above, design and create a picture.

C) Using a sheet of graph paper, use the vocabulary words in letter A to design your own word search puzzle. Exchange with a partner and solve.

Leon's Share

Q & A

Chapter 3

Piece of the Pie

1. When Leon got home from school why did he think it was a special occasion?
2. How do we know that Nana likes to cook?
3. Why did Leon say Nana was the "real boss" in the family?
4. Leon said his grandmother's kitchen was his favorite room. Describe *your* favorite room and tell why you like this room best.
5. Why had Nana baked a pie for Derrick?
6. Should Leon have shared his poem with Nana? Explain
7. Do you think Leon should receive the biggest piece of pie? Explain.

Chapter 3 Activity: *Choose and complete one of the activities below.*

A) Find at least six facts about the state of Louisiana. Share your findings with a partner.

B) Write ten action words from chapter 3 and act them out with a group to see if they can guess your words.

C) Write a news article summarizing the events in chapter three. The following questions should be answered in your article: *Who? What? Where? When? Why? How?*

Leon's Share

Cheater!

1. Why did Derrick's news mean a change for Leon?
2. Nana said, "Now don't go rushin time, Pop." What did she mean?
3. Who gave Nana her "good dishes"? How do you know the dishes were special to her?
4. Do you think Leon is a cheater? Explain.
5. What did Derrick discover about his little brother?
6. Was Leon correct to hide his talent and intelligence? Explain.
7. Do *you* have a special talent or ability no one knows about? Will you ever share it? Explain.

Chapter 4 Activity: *Choose and complete one of the activities below.*

A) Write synonyms for the following words: suddenly, overjoyed, official, complain, console, gradually, confident, beneath. Exchange your list with a partner and write an antonym for each word.

B) Correct the following paragraph and compare with a partner.

Derrick and me looked at each other and quikly returned the everyday plates and glasses back to the cabnet and opened the door of the mahogany curio located in a corner just of the kitchen Their on the bottom shelf was an old worn cardboard box simply marked with the word, dishes? Derrick carefully reached for them and cautiously take them out. Nana had told us the dishes had once belonged to her grate grandmother and had been passed down to her. We knew they were very spechel.

C) Write a letter to Leon telling him why you think he is/is not a cheater. Give good support for your view.

Leon's Share

Q & A

Chapter 5

Coming Clean

1. Why was Leon excited about getting to school early?
2. What would you have done in Leon's place when Mrs. Kelso asked him to sit down? Explain.
3. Describe how Leon and Keith feel about one another.
4. Tell about Leon's thoughts concerning Autumn's seat assignment.
5. Why did Keith accuse Leon of cheating?
6. Why couldn't Leon prove he hadn't cheated on the math assignment?
7. How would you react if you were accused of doing something you hadn't done?

Chapter 5 Activity: *Choose and complete one of the activities below.*

A) Find and list as many nouns as you can from Chapter 5. Compare your list with a partner.

B) Find ten words beginning with the letter "F". Write them in alphabetical order.

C) Make a timeline illustrating the important events in chapter five.

Leon's Share

It's Autumn

1. Why do you think Mrs. Kelso assigned Leon as Autumn's classroom buddy?
2. How did Leon feel about being Autumn's classroom buddy? Explain.
3. How did Autumn feel about Leon being her classroom buddy?
4. Why did the cafeteria suddenly get quiet?
5. Who was Leon expecting to see when he got to Principal Todd's office?
6. How did Leon react to the advice Autumn gave him during the kickball game?
7. Describe Leon's plan to avoid Autumn.
8. Do you agree or disagree with what Leon did? Explain.

Chapter 6 Activity: *Choose and complete one of the activities below.*

A) Write antonyms for the following words: concern, everywhere, found, straight, empty, easy, silent, possible, better, wrong, few, shout, stayed, cry, quiet.

B) Write a poem describing Autumn Tanner. Share your poem with a partner.

C) Find five compound words and use each one in a sentence. Try mixing some of the compounds to make new compound words.

Leon's Share

Sticks and Stones

1. Why do you think Leon took his time going to Principal Todd's office?
2. What captured Leon's attention on his way to the office?
3. How was Leon feeling about the joke he'd told about Autumn.
4. Was Autumn crying because of Leon's joke? Explain.
5. How did Mrs. Buchanan and Principal Todd respond when they found Autumn and Leon?
6. What is a disability?
7. During the meeting in Principal Todd's office, what did Leon think would make the situation better?

Chapter 7 Activity: *Choose and complete one of the activities below.*

A) Complete the Word search puzzle for chapter 7.

B) Make up three questions of your own for chapter 7. Exchange with a partner to answer.

C) Replace each noun with a pronoun. Mrs. Kelso _____ Leon _____ desk _____ Pop's _____ joke _____ Mrs. Buchanan and Autumn_____ Principal Todd_____

D) Choose four nouns from letter C. Write one sentence for each noun and include a pronoun. Example: <u>Autumn (N)</u> was embarrassed so <u>she (P)</u> ran out of the classroom.

Sticks and Stones

```
L   D   T   G   L   H   Y   E   I   O   F   Y   Y   S   R
S   L   I   U   N   C   U   N   K   R   C   L   R   N   T
N   S   F   R   N   I   T   D   U   O   L   D   O   I   T
S   W   E   E   E   E   R   S   D   A   J   N   I   F   N
A   U   G   R   R   C   T   E   I   L   Y   I   V   F   E
G   R   O   V   T   R   T   C   P   T   E   K   A   L   M
U   S   A   V   A   S   E   I   U   M   H   D   H   I   I
E   L   D   T   R   P   I   D   O   N   I   W   E   N   L
S   L   I   O   S   E   G   D   J   N   U   H   B   G   P
S   O   J   E   Y   L   N   E   D   D   U   S   W   P   M
N   G   L   A   N   C   E   D   D   E   I   R   U   B   O
R   E   T   N   E   M   H   S   I   N   U   P   W   A   C
E   V   I   R   R   A   T   T   E   N   T   I   O   N   L
B   R   A   V   E   L   Y   G   O   L   O   P   A   S   Y
R   E   Q   U   E   S   T   S   S   E   R   P   X   E   T
```

APOLOGY ARRIVE ATTENTION AWFUL BEHAVIOR BRAVELY
BURIED   COMPLIMENT   DIRECTION   DISTRESS   ESPECIALLY
EXPRESS FRUSTRATION GLANCED   GUESS HUDDLED
INTERVALS JOKE KINDLY NERVOUS PUNISHMENT
REQUEST SNIFFLING SOIL SUDDENLY UNUSUAL URGENCY

Leon's Share

Chapter 8

Achromatopsia

1. What is Achromatopsia?
2. How did Leon feel about revealing Autumn's disability?
3. Was Principal Todd's decision to keep Leon and Autumn apart the right thing to do? Explain.
4. Why did Leon volunteer to leave Mrs. Kelso's homeroom?
5. Do you think Leon's punishment was too harsh? Explain.
6. What did Leon wish he could do during the meeting with Principal Todd and his grandparents? Why do you think he felt this way?
7. Will Autumn remain Leon's friend? Explain your answer.

Chapter 8 Activity: *Choose and complete one of the activities below.*

A) Complete each sentence using a word from the words provided. (See worksheet on next page).

B) Choose five words from the word box (see worksheet on next page) and write one sentence for each.

C) In a small group, look through magazines and cut out pictures showing examples of friendship. Together work to create a friendship collage. Share when done.

Achromatopsia

Chapter 8

*Choose a word from below to complete each sentence.

1. Leon's _____with Autumn was more important than he realized.

2. Nana had a/an _____on her face that said she disagreed when Pop asked if they would be taking Leon home.

3. Achromatopsia is an example of a _____where color is not seen.

4. Nana and Pop seemed _____when Principal Todd said the word Achromatopsia.

5. Leon _____as he sat in the _____chair.

6. Autumn could not see colors. She was _____.

7. Offering to move to another homeroom _____Leon.

8. Leon _____his hands together to fight his _____ to move.

bewildered separate inwardly speak attempt mahogany
squirmed clasped shocked impulse colorblind disability
relief expression friendship

Leon's Share

The Visit

1. Why was Leon fearful about visiting Autumn's home?
2. Do you agree with Derrick's decision to stay home? Explain.
3. If given the choice, would you have gone with Leon? Explain.
4. To what did Leon compare trying to ring the Tanner's doorbell?
5. How did Leon get the courage he needed to finally ring the doorbell?
6. Describe Autumn's living room.
7. What were Nana and Pop's real names?
8. What surprised Leon about Mr. Tanner?
9. Was Leon satisfied with the outcome of his visit? Explain.
10. Do you think Autumn's request for Leon to invite Keith to play kickball with them was reasonable? Explain.

Chapter 9 Activity: *Choose and complete one of the activities below.*

A) Find six new vocabulary words and define them according to the context used in chapter 9.

B) Unscramble the following words and write one sentence for each one.

laicmex, leshbolmb, nuAtum, irebmemerng, oievc, gratopphoh

C) **Design a poster advertising the main idea of chapter 9. Share your poster.**

Leon's Share

The Return

1. Why did Leon have trouble getting to sleep the night before he returned to class?
2. What did Mrs. Kelso give Leon? Why did she do this?
3. Why did Leon decide not to use his pencil?
4. What did Leon think happened when Autumn didn't show up that morning?
5. Why was Leon surprised by Keith's reaction?
6. When did Leon feel that everything was going to be alright?
7. Why did Leon compare his separation from Autumn to an ocean?

Chapter 10 Activity: *Choose and complete one of the activities below.*

A) Use the clues provided to solve the crossword puzzle (p.25).

B) Complete the chart (p.26) to compare Leon and Autumn. How are they alike?   How are they different?

C) Find five interesting facts about the state of New Jersey. (Suggestions: temperature, state nickname, population, industry, state bird or animal) Write a short paragraph to share your information.

Autumn's Return

Chapter 10

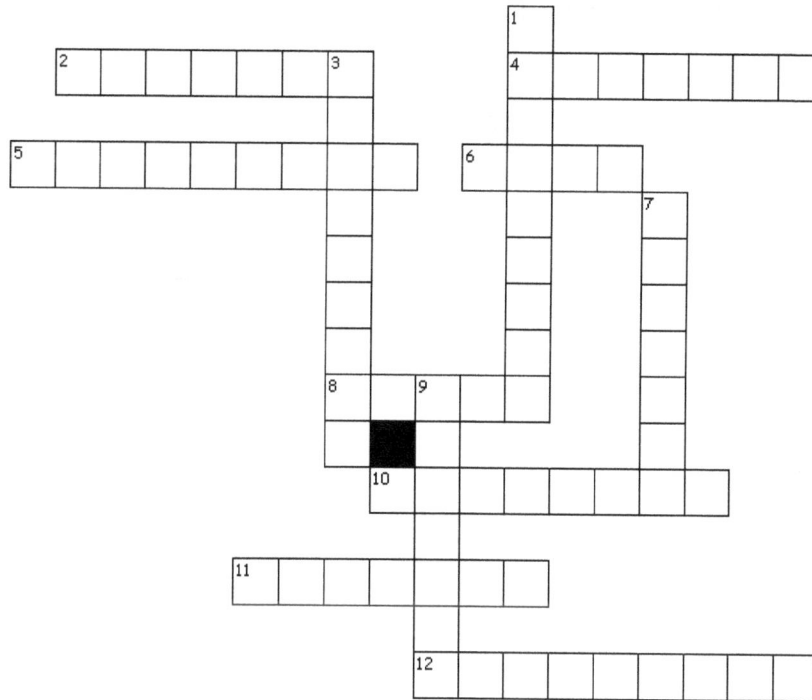

Across

2. Bragged about
4. Bothered
5. morning meal
6. in a kind way
8. Opposite of full
10. school work completed at home
11. real
12. tired

Down

1. Waiting with no complaints
3. Sickened
7. Speak softly
9. To give ones word

Chapter 10

Autumn's Return

Compare Leon and Autumn. How are they alike? How are they different?

Leon Chandler   /   Autumn Tanner

Similarities

_____

_____

_____

_____

_____

_____

_____

_____

Differences

_____

_____

_____

_____

_____

_____

_____

Name_____

Leon's Share

Leon's Share

1. Why didn't Leon hear Nana come into the kitchen?
2. Why do you think Leon didn't tell anyone about his plan?
3. What kind of day was it for Leon?
4. How did Keith react to Leon's invitation?
5. Why do you think Keith stayed silent for so long before he answered Leon's question?
6. Do you think Leon's poem was a good way to show Autumn how he felt? Explain.
7. How did Leon come to believe he had shared something special?

Chapter 11 Activity: *Choose and complete one of the activities below.*

A) Write a letter to the book's author or one of the book's main characters. Ask questions and tell about your favorite part(s) of the story.

B) Work with a small group to prepare a commercial for Leon's Share. Present your commercial.

C) Create a game based on the book. Invite others to play your game.

Name_____

Chapter 11
Leon's Share

*Write a letter to the author or one of the book's main characters. Ask questions and tell about your favorite part(s) of the story. Use the friendly letter format.

_____,

_____

_____

_____

_____

_____

_____

_____

_____

_____

_____

_____

_____

_____,

_____

Other Books
By Mabel Elizabeth Singletary

1. Just Jump!
ISBN: 978-0-8024-2251-4

2. Something To Jump About
ISBN: 978-0-8024-2252-1

3. A Promise and a Rainbow
ISBN: 978-0-8024-2255-2

4. Run, Jeremiah Run!
ISBN: 978-0-8024-2253-8

5. Coming Across Jordan
ISBN: 978-0-8024-2259-0

Available at Mabelesingletary.com

&

online bookstores

ANSWERS

ANSWERS

Chapter 1

Somebody's Got a Secret

1.   Yes he did. As he walked into the classroom, he
     said he strolled through the room like he was loving every
     minute of the attention.

2.   Acceptable answers- Mrs. Kelso is a kind and caring teacher who
     can be firm when she needs to be. (Accept reasonable answers to support response.)

3.   He enjoyed the attention. He knew he could lose his recess, but
     wanting his classmates to laugh seemed more important.

4.   Keith is a very bright student who doesn't get along with Leon.
5.   Accept reasonable answers with an explanation.

6.   Yes, ignoring Leon was the right thing to do. Responding would
     only have gotten Keith in trouble with Mrs. Kelso.

7.   Leon loves and respects his grandfather. He's not sure if his grandfather
     loves him as much as he loves Derrick.

8.   Leon hated disappointing Mrs. Kelso and his grandparents

ACTIVITY   C. at/ten/tion en/cour/age ig/nore laugh/ter mis/be/have se/cret

Chapter 2

A Different Kind of Show

1.   Mrs. Kelso saw each day as brand new. Everyone got a new
     start.
2.   Yes he does. Leon wants to please his grandparents even though he
     lets them down.

3.   He gives the impression that he does not. He doesn't do his homework
     regularly.

4.   He doesn't want to share his poem with his class.
5.   He doesn't know what to expect. It's not like telling jokes.
6.   They don't get along because Keith always beats Leon at everything.
     Keith thinks he's the smartest boy in fifth grade.
7.   He felt good. Mrs. Kelso saw something special about Leon.
8.   Accept reasonable answers with explanation.

Chapter 3

A Piece of the Pie

1. He knew that Nana only baked for special occasions and on Sundays.
2. Leon says that when Nana baked, everything had to be just right. Then she'd say a prayer that The Lord would bless her cooking.
3. Her gumbo would make Pop forget about their disagreement.
4. Leon said his grandma's kitchen was always warm. Responses vary.
5. She was expecting good news about his scholarship.
6. Answers will vary. Accept reasonable explanations to support response.
7. Answers will vary. Accept reasonable explanations to support response.

Chapter 4

Cheater!

1. Leon would have to accept that his brother would be leaving.
2. She meant that time moves very fast without any help.
3. They had been passed on to her from her great-grandmother.
4. Accept reasonable answers and explanations.
5. Derrick discovered that Leon liked to read books.
6. Accept reasonable answers and explanations.
7. Yes/No. Explanations will vary.

Activity

A. (syn.) quickly, delighted, protest, comfort, slowly, self-assured, under, formal.
(ant.) slowly, disappointed, praise, annoy, rapidly, timid, above, informal or relaxed.

B. Derrick and I, quickly, cabinet, off, kitchen., There, dishes., took, great-grandmother, special.

Chapter 5

Coming Clean

1. He planned to share some important news with Mrs. Kelso.
2. Answers will vary.
3. They didn't like one another.
4. He didn't want her there. He preferred the seat stay empty.
5. Keith accused Leon of cheating because of his perfect math paper.
6. He realized he had come into the room when no one else was there.
7. Answers will vary.

Chapter 6

It's Autumn

1. She probably felt Autumn would be a good influence on Leon.
2. Leon didn't want to be Autumn's classroom buddy because she was a girl.
3. Autumn liked Leon and was glad he was her classroom buddy.
4. The students could hear Principal Todd coughing over the loudspeaker.
5. He expected to see his grandparents.
6. He figured she didn't know what she was talking about.
7. He would sit all the way back in the cafeteria where he hoped she wouldn't find him.
8. Accept reasonable explanations.

Chapter 7

Sticks and Stones . . .

1. Leon saw no reason to rush to the principal's office because he knew what to expect. He knew his grandparents would be coming to take him home.

2. He could hear crying coming from around the corner.
3. Leon was feeling bad because he realized he had hurt her badly.
4. No. Autumn was crying because she thought Leon knew her secret.
5. Mrs. Buchanan gave a look of dissatisfaction and said, "Shame on you Leon." Principal Todd insisted Leon come with him and told him his grandparents were on the way.
6. A disability is a physical or mental condition that limits someone's movements, senses, or activities.
7. Leon wanted to tell a joke to make everyone laugh.

(C) Mrs. Kelso/ she
    Leon/he
    Desk/it
    Pop's/his
    Joke/it
    Mrs. Buchanan and Autumn/They
    Principal Todd/he

Chapter 8

Achromatopsia

1. Achromatopsia is colorblindness. One can only see white, black, and gray.
2. He felt bad and wished he could take back what he'd done.
3. Accept reasonable answers.

4. Leon thought if he left, Autumn could stay.
5. Answers will vary.
6. Leon wished he could disappear. Accept reasonable responses.
7. Answers will vary.

ACTIVITY A. Friendship, expression, disability, bewildered, squirmed, mahogany, colorblind, shocked, clasped, impulse

Chapter 9

The Visit

1. Leon didn't know what to expect from Autumn's parents.
2. Answers will vary.
3. Accept reasonable answers.
4. He felt like his feet were glued to the surface of the Tanner's front porch.
5. Nana put her arm around Leon and told him it would be alright.
6. It was a nice comfortable room characterized by peace and warmth.
7. Their real names were Celeste and Warren.
8. Mr. Tanner was pleasant and he shook hands with Leon.
9. Yes, Leon was satisfied knowing that the Tanners were letting Autumn stay in Mrs. Kelso's class.
10. Answers will vary.

ACTIVITY B. exclaim, bombshell, Autumn, remembering, voice, photograph

Chapter 10

Autumn's Return

1. Leon had trouble getting to sleep because he wondered what his classmates would think about him having a girl for a best friend.
2. She gave Leon a "star student" pencil for completing all of his assignments.
3. Leon wanted to save the pencil and use it for something special.
4. Leon thought Autumn's parents had changed their minds and moved her to a different homeroom.
5. Leon was surprised by Keith's reaction because he gave a compliment rather than a criticism.
6. Leon felt everything was going to be alright when he saw Autumn standing next to Mrs. Buchanan at the door of the classroom.
7. Leon compared his separation from Autumn to an ocean because it was wide and deep. To him, it looked like they would never be able to be real friends.

Activity

A. Crossword puzzle- Across (boasted, annoyed, breakfast, nice, empty, homework, exhausted)
Down (patiently, disgusted, whisper, promise)

Chapter 11

Leon's Share

1. Leon didn't hear Nana come into the kitchen because his attention was on the paper he was reading.
2. Accept reasonable answers (Example: He didn't want anyone to try and change his mind. He wanted it to be a surprise.)
3. This was a great day for Leon.
4. At first Keith said nothing, but when he spoke he was happy about the invitation to be on Leon's team.
5. Keith probably stayed silent because he couldn't believe what he was hearing.
6. Answers will vary (Yes, because Leon was able to express himself beautifully through his words.)
7. Leon knew he had done something special when he saw that Nana had baked a pie especially for him.